James B. Kenyon

In realms of golds

James B. Kenyon

In realms of golds

ISBN/EAN: 9783337733353

Printed in Europe, USA, Canada, Australia, Japan

Cover: Foto ©ninafisch / pixelio.de

More available books at **www.hansebooks.com**

IN REALMS OF GOLD

IN

REALMS OF GOLD

BY
JAMES B. KENYON

"Much have I travel'd in the realms of gold."—KEATS.

CASSELL & COMPANY, LIMITED,
739 & 741 BROADWAY, NEW YORK.

CONTENTS.

POEMS AND LYRICS.

	PAGE.
GRAPES OF ESHCOL,	11
PAN,	12
THE ODALIK,	14
THE SATYR'S THEFT,	16
A MEMORY OF THEOCRITUS,	18
REAPING,	20
A MAID OF SICILY,	22
TACITA,	25
IN ARCADY,	27
SHE CAME AND WENT,	29
WHEN CLOVER BLOOMS,	31
ELUSION,	33
ECHO'S LAMENT,	34
DAWN,	36
THE DIFFERENCE,	37
SONG OF THE NORTH WIND,	39
A ROMAN QUEEN,	41
THE KING IS DYING,	44
THE SONG OF BACCHUS,	46
LOVE'S SORCERY,	48
QUATRAIN,	50
THE FAUN,	51
THE BELATED DAFFODILS,	53
REQUIESCAT,	55
A SONG OF THE HILLS,	56
SLEEPYSIDE,	63

CONTENTS.

Mine Adversary,	64
An Old-Fashioned Girl,	66
On the Wheel,	68
An Incomplete Angler,	71
The Tyrian's Memory,	74
Laconia,	77
Risen,	79
Sanbenetto,	81
Daphne,	82
Seed-Time,	84
Harvest,	86
When the Day Declines,	88
Joan d'Arc,	89
In an Old Garden,	91

SONNETS.

A Sea Grave,	95
Vanished,	96
Syrinx,	97
Cleopatra to Antony,	98
Romeo to Juliet,	99
Rizpah,	100
Hagar,	101
Sundered,	102
Crœsus,	103
A City Cry,	104
The Prophet's End,	105
The Traveler,	106
The Angel of Night,	107
Edmund Spenser,	108
Adam,	109

POEMS AND LYRICS

GRAPES OF ESHCOL.

WONDERING they came; they had strange tales to tell
   Of purple hills and valleys half divine,
   Of amber plains which did like morning shine,
And cool, clear springs which ever did upwell.
Wistful they came; and 'twixt them, like a bell,
   Swung downward the dark grapes, the goodly sign
   Of plenty in a land of oil and wine —
The goal of rest to way-worn Israel:
So I, a spy from realms where summer sings
   'Mid billowy fields with radiant blossoms starred,
Bring these the promisers of rarer things
   That wait the coming of the chosen bard —
The shining soul who seeks life's mystic springs,
   And counts no knowledge vain, no journey hard.

PAN.

I'LL seek him yet: in some warm nook
   He lies asleep beside the brook,
Drugged by the spicy gales that pass;
His pipe beside him on the grass
Lies but half trimmed,— just as it fell
When Sleep cast o'er him her soft spell.
I'll seek him yet: he does not hear
The bee that drones beside his ear,
Half buried in the nectared gloom
Of some sweet-burdened, purple bloom.
Above him droop the cooling leaves;
His shaggy bosom falls and heaves,
In his deep slumber's quietness;
He will not hear me, though I press,
Through woven bough and vine and flower,
Quite into his sleep-charmèd bower.
Ah me, how soundly he hath slept!
How well the mossy wood hath kept
Its secret old! The poppied gales,
Blown softly by, have told no tales

PAN.

Of sleeping Pan, while far astray
His white flock goes this many a day.
I'll seek him yet : somewhere he lies
Well screened from peering human eyes ;
And though his hoof-marks, as I know,
From mortal sight passed long ago,
Still I will tread the sylvan aisles
And sunny meadows, miles and miles ;
I'll follow hard the dragon-fly,
As down the stream he circles by ;
I'll track the wild-bee from its home
To that fair place whence it hath come,
Where, hoarding still their honeyed store,
Bloom such rare flowers as starred of yore
The shining slopes of Arcady.
So I will seek him yet ; ah me!
Though human foot hath never trod
The leafy lair where lies the god,
Who knows but by some happy chance
I yet may rouse him from his trance!

THE ODALIK.

BESIDE the fountain's marble brim
    With languid steps she comes to stand;
The snowy swans before her swim,
    And catch the dainties from her hand.

Her arm rests on a porphyry vase,
    And from the long and heavy plumes
Of that rich fan which screens her face
    Float faint and delicate perfumes.

On each slim ankle and white wrist
    The bangles chime like tiny bells;
About her, like an azure mist,
    Her fluttering mantle sinks and swells.

A dreamy music fills the air,
    The fountain tinkles in the sun,
The watchful swans, with stately care,
    Glide slowly past her, one by one.

THE ODALIK.

Her broidered garments round her flow,
   And half reveal the charms they veil;
Within her jetty tresses glow
   The gems that make the sunlight pale.

Her eyes look far away; she heeds
   No longer those who seek her alms —
Not e'en that bolder one who pleads
   With beak against her velvet palms.

Lo, as she stands, what sudden flame
   Is kindled o'er her brow and cheek?
Alas, the memory of her shame!
   She is the favorite odalik.

THE SATYR'S THEFT.

DID'ST thou see him as he fled?
Down this dewy way he sped,
Crashing through the tangled copse,
In a shower of pearly drops
Pattering from the tremulous eaves
Of the pleached and glossy leaves.
See how, in his wild retreat
Through the wood, his flying feet
Crushed the fragile blossoms down;
And those matted shreds of brown
Clinging to yon stunted thorn
From his shaggy vest were torn.
It was in the shady nook,
Where the swift and shallow brook
Spreads abroad its waters clear
In a mimic mountain mere:
Hither she had come to lave
In the cool, pellucid wave;
As she leaned to bathe her face,
Suddenly his rude embrace

THE SATYR'S THEFT.

Compassed her; his hairy arms
Circled all her snowy charms.
O'er his dusky back and side
Her dark locks outfloated wide,
And I caught a fleeting glance
Of her bosom's fair expanse,
And her features scared and white,
As he vanished from my sight.
Vain it were to follow him
Through the forests deep and dim;
Human eye hath never seen,
Human face hath never been,
Where the satyr's lair is made
Far within some sylvan glade.
There the wild bee winds its horn;
There the breezes, morn by morn,
Bring the balm from unknown flowers;
There through all the poppied hours
Golden light lies on the grass,
And the flickering shadows pass;
But no mortal foot shall tread
Where the satyr makes his bed.

A MEMORY OF THEOCRITUS.

THUS will I lie, on this green couch of leaves
    Stript from the wayward vine, and while the brook
Beneath its slender osiers sweetly grieves,
   And elfin echoes haunt each shadowy nook,
      I'll hearken how, among the rocks o'erhead,
      The fountain tinkles down its narrow bed.

Cool in this dim recess the breath of day
   Is softly blown, and from the humid moss
Thin exhalations rise, that steal away,
   Elusive as a dream ; the branches toss
      Their emerald brede above me, and below,
      Far down, the kine to lusher pastures go.

Sweet sounds and odors fold me like a sleep ;
   A wood-bird whistles from its piny bower ;
A maiden's silvery laughter mounts the steep ;
   And dreamily from one tall purple flower
      That o'er me slowly vibrates, censer-wise,
      Fine wreaths of fragrant incense seem to rise.

A MEMORY OF THEOCRITUS.

O singer who, in honeyed Sicily,
  Long years ago upon some morning height,
Did'st hear the droning of the vagrant bee,
  And saw fair Enna smiling in the light,
    I'd half believe thou hadst come back again,
    Should goat-hoofed Pan but pipe a sudden strain.

REAPING.

ALONG the east strange glories burn,
   And kindling lights leap high and higher,
As morning from her azure urn
   Pours forth her golden fire.

From rush and reed, from bush and brake,
   Float countless jeweled gossamers
That glance and dazzle as they shake
   In every breeze that stirs.

A bird, upspringing from the grain,
   Flutes loud and clear his raptured note
That mingles with as blithe a strain
   As e'er thrilled human throat.

Amid the tasseled ranks of corn
   She stands breast-high; her arms are bare;
And round her warm brown neck the morn
   Gleams on her lustrous hair.

REAPING.

The sickle flashes in her hand ;
    The dew laves both her naked feet ;
She reaps and sings, and through the land
    She sends her carols sweet.

The wind breathes softly on her brow;
    To touch her lips tall blossoms seek ;
And as the stricken columns bow,
    They kiss her glowing cheek.

O happy maiden ! in her breast
    Guile hath no place ; her virgin sleep
Vain thoughts ne'er trouble ; she is blest ;
    She hath no tears to weep.

She knows nor longs for prouder things ;
    Her simple tasks are all her care ;
She lives and loves, and reaps and sings,
    And makes the world more fair.

A MAID OF SICILY.

SHE heard the waves creep up the sand;
   Her hair, by roving sea winds blown,
And careless of the prisoning band,
   Down fluttered to the azure zone
     Girt lightly round her perfect form,
     And clasped beneath her bosom warm
   Which like twin lilies shone.

The dew gleamed on her sandaled feet;
   Her clinging robe around her trailed;
Her eyes with morning light were sweet;
   And on her brow, that flushed and paled,
     As love and fear passed o'er her face,
     Was throned a rare and virgin grace,
   Such as earth's dawn first hailed.

A MAID OF SICILY.

Her face was seaward turned; her eyes
   Looked southward, where the amber light
Was mixed with purple in the skies,
   And one fair hand, to shade her sight,
     Against her chaste young brow was raised;
     And so she stood, and seaward gazed
   Across the waters wide and bright.

She saw the level sunrays burn
   Along the midsea's heaving breast;
She saw the circling heavens spurn
   The utmost billow's tossing crest
     Where, on the blue horizon's rim,
     A galley's sails rose, white and dim,
   And all her blood leaped with unrest.

She knows that sail; love's eyes are keen;
   She knows yon dancing bark is his;
From distant coasts where he has been,
   From Cyprus, Tyre, and Tripolis,
     Her lover brings the alien freight
     She prizes not; to those who wait
   More precious is love's first warm kiss.

A MAID OF SICILY.

He homeward brings the costly dyes
   The Romans love, and nard, and myrrh,
And unguents which the Emperor buys,
   And silks, and spice, and fruits which were
     Sun-steeped on far Phœnician hills ;
     But not of these she recks ; love fills
   Alone the happy heart of her.

So let her watch, while clearer rise
   The sails which she has waited long ;
The sun climbs higher up the skies ;
   The sea-wind greets her, salt and strong ;
     Her robe from one white shoulder slips ;
     Her breast is bare ; and from her lips
   Half tremble little waifs of song.

TACITA.

SHE roves through shadowy solitudes,
    Where scentless herbs and fragile flowers
Pine in the gloom that ever broods
    Around her sylvan bowers.

No winds amid the branches sigh,
    No footfall wakes the sodden ground;
And the cold streams that hurry by
    Flow on without a sound.

Strange, voiceless birds from spray to spray
    Flit silently; and all day long
The dancing midges round her play,
    But sing no elfin song.

The haunting twilight ebbs and flows;
    Chill is the night, wan is the morn;
Through this dim wood no minstrel goes,
    No hunter winds his horn.

TACITA.

No panting stag seeks yon dark pool ;
   No shepherd calls his bleating sheep
From sunburnt meads to shadows cool,
   And grasses green and deep.

Across her path, from reed to reed,
   The spider weaves his gossamer ;
She recks not where her footsteps lead,
   The world is dead to her.

Her eyes are sad, her face is pale,
   Her head droops sidewise wearily ;
Her dusky tresses, like a veil,
   Down ripple to her knee.

How many a cycle hath she trod
   Each mossy aisle, each leafy dell !
Alas, her feet with silence shod
   Ne'er flee the hateful spell !

IN ARCADY.

UP from yon myrtle valleys incense curls,
  Blue in the balmy morning; barefoot girls,
With silvery laughter bubbling, like clear rills,
Forth from their dewy lips, trip up the hills,
Brushing the twinkling jewels from the grass,
That scarcely bends beneath them as they pass.
Bright robes that half reveal their budding charms
Flow lightly round them; and their dimpled arms,
That bear in woven baskets fruits and flowers,
Glow in the sunlight. Yonder are the bowers
Of Ceres, to whose shrine these offerings
Of field and grove each happy maiden brings.
And hither also in the smiling morn
Come goodly youths with braided ears of corn,
And stems of purple grapes and pomegranates,
And shining berries, olives, figs and dates.
Now let the dance begin upon the green,
And while the sound of music drifts between
The pleachèd branches of the leafy wood,
Waking sweet echoes in the solitude,

IN ARCADY.

Let twining hands, light feet, and songs and mirth
Be joined, in Ceres praise, to gifts of earth.
And hark! from height to height the shepherds call;
Adown the hill the laughing waterfall
Leaps to the plain ; the bees begin to hum,
And in the glen the partridge beats his drum.
In shady dells, where well the crystal springs,
The naiad laves her limbs and softly sings,
While overhead, from out the oak's thick screen,
The amorous dryad leans to view the scene,
Nor dares to stir a leaf from place, for fear
She sink into the wave and disappear.
Still round the shrine of Ceres, maze on maze,
The dancers featly foot and chant her praise ;
The incense upward floats amid the trees
That o'er them stretch their emerald canopies ;
'Still from the heights the shepherds blithely call
Their bleating flocks ; the jocund waterfall,
Flashing the golden sunlight back again,
Still gambols down to seek the amber plain,
And spread abroad its waters clear and cool
That mimic heaven in an azure pool,
Nigh whose fringed marge a drowsy dragon-fly
Upon a lily-leaf sways dreamily,
And Pan, 'mid rushes and rank water-weeds,
To shape some sweeter pipe, still plucks the reeds.

SHE CAME AND WENT.

SHE came and went, as comes and goes
   The dewdrop on the morning rose,
Or as the tender lights that die
At shut of day along the sky.
Her coming made the dawn more bright,
Her going brought the somber night;
Her coming made the blossoms shine,
Her going made them droop and pine.
Where'er her twinkling feet did pass,
Beneath them greener grew the grass;
The song-birds ruffled their small throats
To swell for her their blithest notes.
But when she went, the blushing day
Sank into silence chill and gray,
The dark its sable vans unfurled,
And sudden night possessed the world.
O fond desires that wake in vain!
She ne'er will come to us again;
And now, like vanished perfume sweet,
Her memory grows more vague and fleet.

SHE CAME AND WENT.

Yet we rejoice that morn by morn
The sad old world seems less forlorn,
Since once so bright a vision came
To touch our lives with heavenly flame,
And show to our bewildered eyes
What beauty dwells in paradise.

WHEN CLOVER BLOOMS.

WHEN clover blooms in the meadows,
    And the happy south winds blow ;
When under the leafy shadows
  The singing waters flow —
    Then come to me ; as you pass
    I shall hear your feet in the grass,
    And my heart shall awake and leap
    From its cool, dark couch of sleep,
    And shall thrill again, as of old,
    Ere its long rest under the mold —
      When clover blooms.

Deem not that I shall not waken ;
  I shall know, my love, it is you ;
I shall feel the tall grass shaken,
  I shall hear the drops of the dew
    That scatter before your feet ;
    I shall smell the perfume sweet
    Of the red rose that you wear,
    As of old in your sunny hair ;
    Deem not that I shall not know
    It is your light feet that go
      'Mid clover blooms.

WHEN CLOVER BLOOMS.

O love, the years have parted —
  The long, long years! — our ways;
You have gone with the merry-hearted
  These many and many days,
    And I with that grim guest
    Who loveth the silence best.
    But come to me — I shall wait
    For your coming, soon or late,
    For soon or late, I know,
    You shall come to my rest below
      The clover blooms.

ELUSION.

A SPIRIT stirs the summer grass,
And whispers to me as I pass;
I catch the gleam of flying feet,
I smell a perfume warm and sweet.

A sudden light, a rustling sound,
Fleet swiftly o'er the dewy ground,
And fade in yonder copse away,
Where lurking shadows cheat the day.

What eye hath seen that dimpled face?
Who yet hath found the secret place,
That refuge in the dim, cool shade,
Where flees and hides the laughing maid?

Ah, happy poet who may guess
The ever-changing loveliness,
The lightsome grace, the airy wiles
Wherewith coy nature masks her smiles,
And, stealing on her unaware,
Behold her when she is most fair!

ECHO'S LAMENT.

HERE in the shadows, on my changeless bed
    Beneath the somber trees, I long have lain ;
Day after day, above my weary head
    The sad leaves rustle, and the chilly rain,
        Slow dripping from each gnarled and twisted bough,
        Shatters its big drops on my flinty brow.

The tangled brakes decay about my feet ;
    The shaggy moss creeps o'er my rigid face :
Afar I hear the young flocks faintly bleat,
    And baying hounds upon the frantic chase ;
        But none make quest for me ; the years go by,
        And still amid these hateful glooms I lie.

Ah ! when the large, cool-breasted Night hath drawn
    Her star-wrought mantle from the waking world,
And on the hills, where gleam the feet of Dawn,
    The trailing banners of the mist are furled,
        Then, O Narcissus, while the woodlands ring,
        Dost thou not miss me by thy silver spring ?

ECHO'S LAMENT.

And when, at noon, on murmurous summer days,
  O'er thymy meadows drone the yellow bees —
When shy wild creatures frisk through leafy ways,
  And fragrant blossoms clasp thy dimpled knees —
    Then, as thou bendest o'er thy fountain clear,
    And look, and yearn, dost thou not wish me near?

Deep in this twilight solitude I dwell,
  And as the languid seasons wax and wane,
I know the thralldom of my stony spell
  Shall ne'er be banished, nor my heart's old pain;
    But O my love, no lightest breeze shall blow
    About thy path that shall not breathe my woe.

DAWN.

THE dews are sifted o'er the lawn;
    Pale vapors fold the shadowy height;
And like a ghost the pallid dawn
    Steals down the aisles of night.

Heaven's myriad torches quench their fires;
    And yonder, o'er the earth's faint rim,
Where in the mist the moon expires,
    The morning star grows dim.

The soft sleep-angel's dusky plumes
    Glimmer along the silent way
She takes to lands of dreamful glooms,
    Far from the garish day.

The hill-tops flush — the night is done;
    A sudden bird-note, sweet and strong,
Rings out, till lo! beneath the sun
    The world is drenched with song.

THE DIFFERENCE.

HER plants bloom on the window ledge;
    Behind its wicker bars
Her bird still sings, and by yon hedge
    Her lilies burn like stars.

Beside the walk her pansies raise
    Their faces to the sun,
And round her porch, in many a maze,
    The flickering vine-leaves run.

Her slender wheel has ceased to hum
    Beneath her nimble hands,
And there, close-shut and sadly dumb,
    Her sweet-voiced spinet stands.

The doves still flutter to her door,
    And wait and coo in vain;
And passers-by pause as of yore
    To hear her happy strain.

THE DIFFERENCE.

But she who, like a fine perfume,
  Filled all the sunny place,
Lies in a hushed and darkened room,
  With pale and moveless face.

SONG OF THE NORTH WIND.

HARK to the voice of me!
Hear thou the singing
Of him who has never
Been paid for his song!
This is the choice of me,
Still to go ringing
The rhymes that forever
Are surly and strong.

Know'st thou the regions cold
Whence I have hasted?
Know'st thou the way I take
Over the earth?
Still stand the legends old —
Ice-kings unwasted —
Fending the frigid lake
Where I had birth.

SONG OF THE NORTH WIND.

Frost-banded fountains
Snow-fed from far peaks ;
Firths of the polar sea
Rigid as stone ;
Shag-bearded mountains ;
Deeps that no star seeks ;
Strange lights that solar be —
These I have known.

Men fear the breath of me ;
Sorrow and anguish,
Famine and fever
Follow my path.
I am the death of thee ;
I make thee languish ;
Swiftly I sever
Love's ties in my wrath.

Chains can not hold me,
Gyves can not bind me,
Bolts can not lock me,
 Floods can not drown !
Fly — and I fold thee ;
Hide — and I find thee ;
Cry — and I mock thee,
Howling thee down !

A ROMAN QUEEN.

IMPERIOUS on her ebon throne
   She sits, a queen, in languid ease;
Her lustrous locks are loosely blown
   Back from her brow by some stray breeze
Lost in that vast, bright hall of state,
Where thronging suppliants fear and wait.

A dreamy fragrance, fine and rare,
   Of sandal, nard and precious gum,
With balmy sweetness fills the air,
   And mingles with the incense from
A quaint and costly azure urn,
Where Indian spices ever burn.

A jeweled serpent, wrought in gold,
   Coils round her white and naked arm;
Her purple tunic, backward rolled,
   Reveals the full and regal charm
Of her fair neck, and ivory breast,
Half veiled beneath her broidered vest.

A ROMAN QUEEN.

Her eyelids droop upon her eyes,
   And curtained by the silken lash,
The smouldering fire that in them lies
   Is scarcely seen, save when a flash,
Like that which lights the polar snow,
Gleams from the dusky depths below.

Her proud, cold lips are lightly wreathed
   In smiles, as if with high disdain
She scorns to show her hate is sheathed,
   And that he sues not all in vain
For favors of her haughty will,
Or e'en love's rarer guerdon still.

He stands before her white and fierce ;
   His bosom with swift passion shakes ;
His burning vision seeks to pierce
   Her very soul ; he pleads ; he wakes
Within her heart a wild desire,
That flames and mounts like sudden fire.

A subtle glance, a whispered word,
   A waving of her perfumed hand,
He feels his secret prayer is heard —
   That she will know and understand ;
The queen is hid, and for a space
A love-swayed woman holds her place.

A ROMAN QUEEN.

He bows, he leans toward the throne;
   Her breath is warm upon his cheek;
She murmurs, and in every tone
   He hears the love she dares not speak;
What though the surging hundreds press?
No eye shall see her swift caress.

Let him beware; he toys with fate;
   False as the glittering serpent is
On her white arm, her love to hate
   Shall change eftsoons; then every kiss
She gives him with her fickle breath
Shall be surcharged with secret death.

THE KING IS DYING.

FOOL, stand back, the king is dying,
    Give him what little air remains ;
See'st thou not how his pulse is flying?
    Hear'st thou not how he gasps and strains
To catch one other stertorous breath?
God! how he labors! yes, this is death!

Blow up the fire—his feet are cold ;
    Ay, though a king, he can not buy
One briefest moment with all his gold;
    His hour has come, and he must die ;
Withered and wrinkled, and old and gray,
The king fares out on the common way.

Light the tapers ; he's almost gone ;
    Stir, thou fool, 'tis past the hour
To cower and cringe, and flatter and fawn —
    The thing lying there is shorn of power;
Henceforth the lips of the king are dumb :
Bring up thy ghostly viaticum.

THE KING IS DYING.

Absolve his soul ; need enough, God wot !
    Mumble and sprinkle and do thy shriving ;
Yet, methinks, here and there shall be left a blot,
    Hideously foul, despite thy striving ;
Nor purfled quilts, nor pillows of lace,
Can relieve the guilt in that grim old face.

Soft ! stand back — it is his last ;
    Get hence, thy priestly craft is o'er ;
For him the pomp of the world is past —
    The king that was is king no more :
Let the bells be rung, let the mass be said,
And the king's heir know that the king is dead.

THE SONG OF BACCHUS.

COME, satyrs, from the arbored vine;
    Silenus, leave the shady wood;
  And quit, O Pan, the reedy flood,
And those shrill, silly pipes of thine.

Ho! shepherds, leave beside the spring
    The chaste, cold nymph; and on the hill
    Thy nibbling flocks let rove at will;
Come down to laugh, and dance and sing.

Here lissome maids, with lifted arms
    And dangled clusters, lightly trip;
    Here laughter wreathes each rosy lip;
Here beauty half unveils her charms.

Ye know me well; my stainèd mouth,
    My rounded limbs, my tangled hair,
    My supple body, smooth and fair,
My cheeks like summers of the south;

THE SONG OF BACCHUS.

I am the vintage god ; I go
   Where'er the grape's blood gurgles through
   The fat-ribbed press. O merry crew,
Come while the purple vats o'erflow!

LOVE'S SORCERY.

WHERESOE'ER thou goest, Sweet,
Peace shall go before thy feet;
Forth shall gush the song of bird,
And the blossoms, faintly stirred,
Shall breathe incense, fine and rare,
On the love-enchanted air.
Round thy pathway, for thy sake,
From the ground a light shall break,
And thy footsteps shall be set
With the mint and violet.
Greener hills shall slope away
Where the mild-eyed cattle stray;
Fairer skies shall arch thee o'er
Than the world hath known before.
Not a fear shall shake thy heart;
Spent shall be Grief's venomed dart
Ere it reach thee; thou shalt go
Where life's crystal fountains flow.

LOVE'S SORCERY.

For a wizard, wondrous wise,
Round thee weaves his sorceries,
And the earth shall changed be
By his sovereign alchemy.
Thou to nature shalt be dear;
Subtlest music thou shalt hear
In the sounds of gurgling springs,
And the faery chime that rings
Where the grasses, cool and wet,
Screen the glimmering rivulet.
Thou shalt hear, o'er pleasant leas,
Slumberous murmurings of the bees,
And the grasshopper's shrill tune,
Through the long bright afternoon.
Night shall bring the healing dews;
And the viewless hand that strews
Precious balm of Paradise
On the flowers' closed eyes
Shall with silken touches woo
Thee Sleep's rosy portals through.

Howsoe'er the seasons fleet,
Kindly stars shall o'er thee meet;
Love shall minister to thee,
And thy life shall charmèd be.

QUATRAIN.

SHE would not stir a single jetty lash,
  To hear me praised; but when my life was blamed
Her parian cheeks were kindled like a flash,
  And from her heart a sudden love upflamed.

THE FAUN.

I CHANCED upon him in the early morn;
   He stood beneath the vine-roofed trellises,
   All heedless of the yellow-belted bees
That fumed about him; in the ripened corn
   The reapers sang, and through the grove of pine
   A clear-voiced neatress called her straying kine.

With osier crates poised on their heads, and bare
   Brown necks and dimpled shoulders all aglow,
   The vintage-girls were passing to and fro
Along the dewy slope; the morning air
   With sudden laughter rang, and on the steep
   The frolic echoes wakened from their sleep.

I caught the twinkling of his hairy ears;
   I heard his eager murmurs, as he plucked
   The purple clusters, and the nectar sucked
From wine-red cores; his ever-watchful fears
   Were drowned a moment in the mad delight
   Wherewith he reveled in my wondering sight.

THE FAUN.

He stood tiptoe and stretched his naked arm
  To draw the heavy-fruited branches near ;
  I saw him crush the glossy orbs, and smear
His cheeks with crimson ; then in wild alarm
  He heard my stealthy footsteps, and amid
  The wattled vines he swiftly fled and hid.

He scarcely snapped a bind-weed in his flight,
  Or frailest tendril; long I sought in vain
  Through leafy glooms, but found him not again :
The dew dried on the grass, the mellow light
  Brimmed all the misty valley, but the faun,
  Fleet as a vision of the morn, was gone.

THE BELATED DAFFODILS.

WAKE, sister daffodilly, wake!
    The buds their barren slumbers break;
The trailing willow, by the stream,
Roused from its long and wintry dream,
Shakes all its silken tassels free.
The robin's jocund minstrelsy,
And early bluebird's velvet note,
About the fields and orchards float.
No more the hurtling March winds pass,
But low, sweet sounds of growing grass,
Of rustling herb and tender flower,
Rise from the green turf hour by hour.
Wake, sister daffodilly, lo,
From out the south mild breezes blow;
Along the wood-paths, warm and wet,
Springs up the frail wood-violet.
Already from its soft brown bed
The crocus lifts its dowsy head,
And stares with slow and wondering eyes
Into the changeful April skies.

THE BELATED DAFFODILS.

Wake, sister, here 'tis damp and dark;
Leap from thy chilly couch, and hark
How peal the waxen lily-bells,
To call us from our gloomy cells.
Too long hath slumber sealed our eyes;
Our mates have risen; let us rise
And take from hence our upward flight;
Let us go seek the pleasant light.
The cattle browse upon the hill;
The blossoms nod beside the rill;
The bee darts by on vagrant wing;
The birds from dewy copses sing;
And in fresh closes, to and fro,
The whistling plowmen blithely go.
Dear sister, from these chambers cold,
Beneath the damp and gloomy mold,
Where winter-tranced we long have lain,
We'll flee to seek the light again.
Dost see the day, dear, as we rise?
Hark to the insects' mellow cries!
Ah me, how sweet the south's warm breath!
How fair is life! how dark is death!
Lo, all the world is bourgeoning,
And this, dear sister, this is Spring!

REQUIESCAT.

SHE sleeps, and may her peaceful rest
    Unbroken be;
The flowers that nod above her breast
    She can not see;
To warbling bird, to purling brook,
    Deaf are her ears;
Sealed is the volume of the book
    Of her brief years.
So let her rest; she will not heed
    The tales they tell;
She recks not now of word or deed —
    She slumbers well.

A SONG OF THE HILLS.

FRONTING the wide-browed east they stand;
 Slowly beneath God's mighty hand
They rose and took their shape; the dews
Distill upon them; heavenly blues,
And rainbow purples, from which lean the stars,
Lightly o'erarch them; down their rugged scars
 Pour balms of dark and light.
 How fair the sight
Of cliff and glen, of oak and pine,
And ever-upward clambering vine,
And long green sweep of brambly slope!
Where slanting sunbeams shyly grope
Through leafy screens, along its bed
Of moss, 'twixt gnarlèd roots, with stealthy tread
The cold stream seeks the vale.
Here, while the heavens yet are pale,
On her wide altars morning burns
Her mystic incense: through the ferns,
And flowers, and creepers, and thick boughs,

A SONG OF THE HILLS.

Old Nature's truest devotees
    Send up their matin vows
    And vesper harmonies,
      Day after day.
From every dew-plashed spray,
From blooms where linger long the plundering bees,
  From frail herbs crushed by careless feet,
  And buds scarce breathed on by the breeze,
  Exhale rare odors, fine and fleet.

Here, where the night and the morn first meet,
Are myriad melodies, wonderful, sweet.
Hark! how the heart of the dawn doth beat!
Whisperings, stirrings, rustling of wings,
Sounds like swift fingers swept o'er a harp's strings —
Sounds shot with silence, with silence that groweth,
That round through the aisles and the dim arches
    floweth
Like a stream lapping low, laughing loud 'mid the
    grasses;
    Till suddenly passes
A spirit that hushes one instant the breath
Of the earth and the sky to the stillness of death —
One instant a pause in the pulse of the dawn,—
One instant the joy of awaking withdrawn.

A SONG OF THE HILLS.

      O moment supreme
      'Twixt waking and dream,
      'Twixt longing intense
      And throbbing suspense!
But listen! the liquid, soft note of a bird
Wakes the world from its spell, then another is heard,
Till lo, with a crash, from the sky and the ground
Bursteth a tempest of musical sound!
      O fear, thou hast fled!
      Thou, silence, art dead!
Thou, joy, hast awaked from the thralldom of sleep,
And the dark tides of sorrow are turned back to the
    deep.

      Lay thine ear to the earth
      And hearken what mirth
Through fairy-land riots because of the birth
Each moment of flowers and fair green things,
And the mystic unsealing of magical springs
      In the heart of the hills!
      What rapture thrills
Through the roots and stems of the braided weeds,
And quivers and shivers amid the reeds
      That watch by the streams,
      Because from their dreams

A SONG OF THE HILLS.

In the womb of the dark have been wakened to light
The souls of new plants to people the height.

      Here trade shall not come,
      And the voice shall be dumb
Of hard-hearted Thrift; yea, even the stroke
Of the ax that is laid to the root of the oak
  Shall sound muffled and far:
      For barter and gain
      Belong to the plain,
      And there they shall bide,
      Whatever betide.
  Here the wheels can not jar
Of commerce that thunders and shrieks on its way,
But the tremulous shadows fantastically play
Through bickering leaves, and small black eyes
Twinkle from glooms where the dewberry lies,
And the garrulous squirrel, and the finch, and the jay
Gossip the fleet-footed summer away.
And here from the pearlèd fields of morn,
On the viewless wings of the winds are borne
Perfumes sweeter than nard or myrrh.
O pungent fragrance of pine and fir!
What delicate scents from the indolent east,
That are shed for the Sultan, as he sits at his feast,

A SONG OF THE HILLS.

Can vie with the balsam's resinous breath
To quench in the blood the fierce fever of death?

    Hark! while the dusk's pale curtain falls,
    Across the dim gray upland calls
    The twilight-loving whip-poor-will.
    O night, brood softly o'er the hill!
    Fair night, your vast star-spaces fill
    With tender lights that shall not wane
    Till morn shall wake the world again.
    Thus, in the shadow of God's hand,
    While o'er the sky the dark is fanned,
    Upon the hill-top let me stand.
    How near is heaven! how near each star!
    The noisy world how far! how far!
    O soul, for flight thy wings expand;
    Look yonder to the promised land;
    From such a height, with fond desire,
    Ere from the earth, in clouds of fire,
    The ancient seer was rapt away,
    He looked and saw the starry dome
    And kindled glories of God's home,
        Nor wished to stay.
    O height! O height! thrice-blessed height!
    Upon thee calmly rest the night,
    And sweetly break the morning's light

A SONG OF THE HILLS.

Above thee ;
He who would flee the world's vain strife,
And find a larger, nobler life,
    Must love thee.

SLEEPYSIDE.

PILED against the turquoise sky
    Pearl-white banks of vapor lie ;
Lazily a fickle breeze
Creeps along the dappled leas.
Midway of the sleepy stream,
Ruminating as they dream,
Stand the drowsy-lidded kine,
Shaded by a clambering vine.
On the gray roofs of the town
The high summer sun looks down ;
Grass is growing in the street,
Where tanned reapers, with bare feet,
Faring fieldward slowly pass,
Or some brown, slim-ankled lass,
Loitering dreamily along,
Hums a half-forgotten song.
From the latticed porches come
Breaths of honeysuckle bloom ;
Sunflowers doze beside the wall ;
On the rick the sparrows call,

SLEEPYSIDE.

Here no sounds of sordid strife
Fret the peaceful ways of life;
Steeped in languor are the days,
As yon slopes are steeped in haze;
Heeded less the passing hours
Than the sunshine on the flowers —
Than the bee with dusty thighs
That across the meadow flies,
Pouncing like a burly lover
On a nodding crimson clover.
Somewhere 'mid the shadows deep
Time has fallen fast asleep,
And his idle scythe and glass
By him lie upon the grass;
Thus forever let him bide
In thy thralls, O Sleepyside.

MINE ADVERSARY.

THOU mine adversary art,
 Thou, love, that with ruthless dart
Didst so sorely wound my breast.
Lo, thou camest as a guest,
And as such I welcomed thee
To my hospitality.
My poor roof I bade thee share,
Bade thee taste my frugal fare —
Amber honey, wine and bread;
And when thou hadst supped, I led
Thee to my warm ingle-nook,
Cheering thee with song and book.
Thou my welcome didst betray;
Thou my kindness didst repay,
Caitiff-like, with swift despite :
For, in silence of the night,
When the darkness was most deep,
And the world was hushed in sleep,
Thou didst rise to do me wrong;
Thou didst bind me fast and strong.

MINE ADVERSARY.

And while thus I helpless lay,
Thou didst steal my peace away,
Thou didst rob me of my joy,
Thou didst make my heart thy toy —
As a target for thy skill,
Thou didst pierce it at thy will;
And whene'er I prayed to thee,
Thou didst mock my misery.
Now I have escaped thy hands;
Sundered are thy silken bands;
Thou shalt never vex me more —
Lo, I spurn thee from my door.
Pass! henceforth I'll none of thee;
Let thy ways be far from me;
For howe'er the years may go,
Thou shalt be my dearest foe.

AN OLD-FASHIONED GIRL.

OLD-FASHIONED? Yes, I must confess
The antique pattern of her dress,
The ancient frills and furbelows,
The faded ribbons and the bows.
Why she should show those shrunken charms,
That wrinkled neck, those tawny arms,
I can not guess; her russet gown
Round her spare form hangs loosely down;
Her voice is thin and cracked; her eye
And smile have lost their witchery.
By those faint jests, that flagging wit,
   By each attenuated curl,
She surely is, I must admit,
   An odd, old-fashioned girl.

'Tis long, long since she had a beau,
And now with those who sit a-row
Along the wall she takes her place,
With something of the old-time grace.

AN OLD-FASHIONED GIRL.

She yearns to join the mazy waltz,
And slyly sniffs her smelling-salts.
Ah, many an angel in disguise
May walk before our human eyes!
Where'er the fever smitten lie
In grimy haunts of poverty,
Along the dark and squalid street,
 Mid drunken jests of boor and churl,
She goes with swift and pitying feet —
 This same old-fashioned girl.

ON THE WHEEL.

HOW fair they lie!—the circling hills,
Down whose green slopes the summer spills
Her lavish wealth of sun and rain,
Of light and dew. Along the plain,
The errant spice-winds, breathing balm
And scent of southern pine and palm,
Whisper amid the rustling corn
That shakes its plumes beneath the morn.
Through grassy closes, clear and bright
The brooks dance in the misty light,
And one blithe bird, loud caroling,
Dips in the flood a glancing wing.
The flowers that bloom beside the way,
The glistening hedge, the thorny spray,
And myriad beaded blades of grass
Sparkle with diamonds as we pass.
Hark! from the field the farmer's song,
And answering echoes, sweet and long,
Redouble round the emerald vale,
Till o'er the wold they faint and fail.

ON THE WHEEL.

Still as we pass on noiseless wheels,
The changing landscape glows and reels;
The flaming sun, high and more high,
Mounts up the cloudless summer sky;
We catch the shouts of lads at play
Amid the fragrant new-mown hay,
And sounds of shrill-voiced grigs that sing,
And whetted scythes that cheerly ring.
Through many a shifting scene we flash:
We hear the busy mill-wheel dash;
We hear the shaft that creaks and groans,
The ceaseless whirring of the stones;
Then on we fare; the clattering mill
Is left behind, and all is still.
Ay, all is still; high noon o'erhead
A poppied influence hath shed;
The very insects cease to hum,
And all the breathless world is dumb.

Still on with noiseless wheels we go,
Till in the west the sun dips low —
Till whip-poor-wills begin to call,
And o'er the fields slim shadows fall.
Along our way the midges spin;
Hushed is the day's melodious din,

ON THE WHEEL.

While piping voices, far and near,
With sweet lamenting vex the ear.
The forest aisles are still and dark,
Save where the fire-fly lights his spark;
And o'er the marish by the way
A mist is rising, ghostly gray.
Now softly glows the evening star
Above us; we have ridden far,
And night is come; a sound of bells,
Like sudden music, sinks and swells
In yonder vale, and through the night
A lamp shines like a beacon-light.
Ah, happy inn! ah, happy guest!
How sweet is night! how sweet is rest!

AN INCOMPLETE ANGLER.

THE bearded grass sways to and fro,
As o'er the fields light zephyrs go;
The reeds nod by the river's brink,
Where birds come down to lave and drink ·
Upon the wave the lilies ride;
The trailing vines dip in the tide;
And countless frogs, screened in the sedge,
Boom all along the water's edge.
Here, where the shadows round me wait,
I'll sit and cast my luring bait.
Above my leafy canopy
The summer clouds float dreamily;
The sun, high o'er the cool dark wood,
Smiles down upon the twinkling flood;
The busy insects round me hum;
The stealthy herons go and come;
A butterfly, with gorgeous wings,
To yon tall flag one moment clings,

AN INCOMPLETE ANGLER.

Then with a sidewise wavering flight,
Rises and flutters out of sight.
Still I my luckless victim bide :
I watch where frolic sunbeams hide
Deep in the bosom of the stream ;
I see his burnished armor gleam,
As round and round the tempting fly
He circles oft and warily.
Why should a fish refuse to dine
From such a dainty hook as mine?
I'll wait and watch him yet. Ah me!
The day is warm. How drowsily
The flies drone near! The river flows
Like sluggish Lethe ; I shall doze
If nature thus my senses steep
In languor — but . . I . . must . . not . . sleep.

*   *   *   *   *   *

Old fellow, are you waiting yet
To taste my hook ? . . The grass is wet !
How now — the dew is falling ? No ! . .
Yes, in the west the sun is low,
And shadows lie around me deep :
It must be that I dropped asleep.
O Isaak Walton—honored ghost ! —
Didst e'er thus slumber at thy post ?

AN INCOMPLETE ANGLER.

But see, the fireflies round me flit!
I wonder if that rascal bit :
The hook is gone ! . . . and snell gone too !
There's nothing further left to do,
But meekly wind my idle reel,
And homeward fare with empty creel.

THE TYRIAN'S MEMORY.

WHAT stars were kindled in the skies,
    What blossoms bloomed, what rivers ran,
I know not now; how wide the span
    Of years which dimly stretch between
That morn I saw the big sun rise,—
    Blinking upon the dazzling sheen
Of banners in the Grecian van,—
    And this, no tongue shall tell, I ween.

On helm and shield, on sword and spear,
    The sun shone down exultingly;
No son of Tyre knew how to flee
    Before the face of any foe,
Nor would our women shed a tear,
    Though face to face with speechless woe,
And heart to heart with misery;
    For *fear* a Tyrian could not know.

THE TYRIAN'S MEMORY.

There came the sound of clashing arms,
    Of catapults and falling stones,
    Of shouts and shrieks, and stifled groans,
        While men stood on the crumbling wall,
And recked not of the dire alarms,
        But saw their brave compatriots fall
    And heard the crunching of their bones,
        Then closed with death, unheeding all.

I know not how the battle fared,
    Though Tyre, "the ocean queen," is dead,
    And lowly lies her crownless head,
        Amid the ashes of her pyre.
Few were the warriors that were spared
        The spear, the flying dart, the fire;
    Into my heart an arrow sped —
        My eyes were closed on falling Tyre.

I have forgot how tenderly
    The olive ripened on the hill;
    How sweetly, when the nights were still,
        The nightingale sang in the grove;
How soft the moon was on the sea,
        How low the mourning of the dove;
    For my dead heart no memories thrill,
        Save the glad memory of my love.

THE TYRIAN'S MEMORY.

O, like the footsteps of the morn
 Her footsteps gleamed along the street ;
 Her shining, foam-white, sandaled feet
  Fell lightly as the summer rain
On stones which grosser feet had worn ;
  And, but my heart so long has lain
  In ashes, it would wake and beat
   At thought of meeting her again.

Her hair was dark as Egypt's night ;
 Her breasts shone like twin nenuphars ;
 Her brave eyes burned like Syrian stars
  That morn she pressed her lips to mine,
And bade me forth unto the fight ;
  My blood shot through my veins like wine ;
  I felt myself another Mars —
   In thew, in life, in love divine.

Who knows that on the emerald zone
 Which belts the changeless azure sea
 Another city yet may be,
  More fair than Tyre ? Nathless, I wis,
Howe'er the phantom years have flown,
  The wrinkled world must ever miss
  That Tyrian maid who gave to me
   Her first, her last, her farewell kiss.

LACONIA.

B.C. 480.

BENEATH the summer stars they part;
  No weak and unavailing tear
Shall from her down-dropt lashes start,
  In token of the nameless fear,
The hopeless pain, the bitter smart,
That storm the white gates of her heart.

Dark braided tresses, soft and fine;
  Sweet eyes that love hath made more sweet;
Warm, dimpled lips as red as wine;
  And in the sward her naked feet,
Half hid by woven flower and vine,
Pale through the balmy darkness shine.

The glimmering dew is on the grass;
  The distant sea moans in the night;
The vagrant breezes sigh and pass;
  The wattled flocks bleat on the height;
But naught can charm them now; alas,
Earth is not fair as once it was!

LACONIA.

For they must part; beyond the hills,
   Beyond the blue Corinthian sea,
Past Dorian steeps that flash with rills,
   O'er vine-clad fields of Thessaly,
He fares to where the war-cry thrills,
Where courage dies, and hatred kills.

His heart is brave; he loves his land;
   He answers valor's high behest;
But, oh! he loves the warm white hand
   He holds against his aching breast.
Ah, 'twixt what thorny ways they stand!
How stern is duty's swift command!

A kiss, a sigh, a low farewell;
   He fades into the misty dark,
And faint and fainter down the dell
   His footsteps fall: she waits to hark —
While in her heart strange passions swell —
How from the wood grieves Philomel.

RISEN.

ERE yet the shadowy mountain tops
    Were silvered with the light,
Or off the lilies slipped the drops
    Won from the dewy night;
Ere yet the morning's incense curled
    O'er glimmering Galilee,
The grave had yielded to the world
    Its awful mystery.

Through all the night the pallid stars
    Watched trembling o'er the tomb,
And Olivet wrapped all its scars
    Deep in the fragrant gloom;
The world one instant held its breath,
    When from the flashing heaven
God's angel swept, more strong than death,
    And death's dark bonds were riven.

RISEN.

Forth from the sepulcher's embrace
   Behold the Conqueror come!
O morning sun, unveil thy face!
   O earth, no more be dumb!
From century to century
   The pæan now shall ring —
O grave, where is thy victory?
   O death, where is thy sting?

SANBENETTO.

AND will ye clothe us thus in shame?
    Think ye the scarlet vestures meet?
Shall they not perish in the flame
    That shall be kindled at our feet?

Yea, shall these hateful robes withstand
    The fiery floods that, high and higher,
Shall round us roll, as with fierce hand
    Ye thrust the roaring fagots nigher?

Or, who shall say that — while ye cry
    " Down, Antichrist!" and mock the sight
Of our last sufferings — as we die,
    These may not change to robes of light?

DAPHNE.

"WHICH way went she? Hast thou seen
  Any signs where she hath been?
Hast thou marked the trembling grass
Droop where her light feet did pass?
By this woodside did she glide?
In the nooks where she might hide —
In the dingle, in the dell —
Hast thou sought the maiden well?
Haply down the path she fled
Thou mayst find a tell-tale shred
From some bramble fluttering still,
Or beside the shrunken rill,
Where she crossed it at a bound,
Spy her footprints on the ground.
Somewhere she hath stayed her flight;
In some thicket, couched from sight
On brown needles of the pines,
Laughing softly, she reclines.
Listen! didst thou hear o'erhead,
Where the bay's wide branches spread,

DAPHNE.

Silver accents faintly fall
Like a murmur musical?
Daphne, cease thy vain elusion;
Leave, my love, thy shy seclusion;
Come whence thou art deftly hiding,
Come, nor fear Apollo's chiding."
In the laurel's shade he stood,
And his cry rang through the wood.

Then amid the leaves above
Sighed a gentle voice : " O love,
Go thy way — thy search is o'er,
Thou mayst never see me more;
And though, prisoned in this tree,
I can never come to thee,
From Apollo's fierce endeavor
I shall rest secure forever."

SEED-TIME.

THE fields lie swathed in misty blue;
   Dim vapors crown the wooded height;
From every trembling spray the dew
   Shoots back the morning's quivering light.
In hollows where the tender fern
Uncurls beside the glimmering burn
The cool gray shadows linger yet,
To kiss the pale young violet.
Hark! singing through the orchard close,
   And whistling o'er the furrowed plain,
The lusty sower blithely goes
   To drop the golden grain.

Clear morning sounds are in the air;
   The birds their jocund matins swell;
Each stream makes music fine and rare;
   Each fountain rings its crystal bell.
Sweet from the blooming apple-trees,
Come elfin quirings of the bees,

SEED-TIME.

And from far uplands, faintly borne,
Float mellow greetings to the morn.
O tuneful world! each wind that blows
   Brings from the field a glad refrain,
Where, singing still, the sower goes
   And drops his golden grain.

HARVEST.

THE hills are steeped in slumberous haze;
    The wind is breathing soft and low;
On tranquil slopes the cattle graze;
    Through twinkling light the waters flow.
About the meadows, smoothly shorn,
The cricket winds his cheery horn,
And o'er the calm expanse of sky
The filmy clouds drift lazily.
Across the smiling valley — hark!
    How steals the echo, sweet and long,
Of those who sing from morn till dark
    The happy harvest song.

The mossy barns, with heapèd floors,
    Amid the peaceful landscape lie;
The doves wheel through the open doors;
    About the eaves the swallows fly.
Now slowly rolls the creaking wain
Up from the yellow fields of grain,

HARVEST.

Where swart-armed reapers gayly sing,
And sturdy sickles glance and ring.
O liberal earth ! O fruitful days !
  Each wind that stirs the rustling leaves
Bears round the world the grateful praise
  Of those who bind the sheaves.

WHEN THE DAY DECLINES.

WHEN the day declines,
    And the night is near —
When the low sun shines
    On the landscape sere —
Then, while shadows creep
    Over vale and height,
Lo! beyond the deep
    A single star grows bright.

When my life declines,
    And the night is near —
When the low sun shines
    On a way of fear —
Then, while shadows creep
    O'er my glimmering sight,
Lo! beyond the deep
    May a star grow bright.

JOAN D'ARC.

ONCE in the fields she watched her peaceful flocks;
    Light were her feet upon the sunny hills;
For her the violets smiled beside the rocks;
    Hers was the silver music of the rills.

She breathed fine odors from the woody place
    Where cool, deep ferns were set; above her head
The summer sky leaned like a tender face;
    Along her path the morning dews were shed.

But suddenly she heard the wild alarm
    Of deadly war; then from her simple sheep,
Forth to the conflict and the battle's harm
    She went like one awaking from a sleep.

Ah! when the flames rolled round her in the mart,
    And cruel faces wavered through the haze
Of her fierce martyrdom,— when on her heart
    Thronged the swift memories of other days,—

JOAN D'ARC.

Perchance no thought of royal pomp and pride,
  No thought of armies, nor of iron war's
Torn fields, nor of the men who fought and died,
  Nor yet of stony cells nor prison bars,—

No thought of these was hers ; but on her ears
  Faint sounds of sheep-bells smote, as in a dream,
And a fair vision glimmered through her tears —
  Her father's cottage by a quiet stream.

IN AN OLD GARDEN.

DOWN this pathway, through the shade,
Lightly tripped the dainty maid.
In her eyes the smile of June,
On her lips some old sweet tune.
Through yon ragged rows of box,
By that awkward clump of phlox,
To her favorite pansy bed,
Like a ray of light, she sped.
Satin slippers, trim and neat,
Gleamed upon her slender feet;
Round her ankles, deftly tied,
Ribbons crossed from side to side.
Here her pinks, old-fashioned, fair,
Breathed their fragrance on the air;
There her fluttering azure gown
Shook the poppy's petals down.
Here a rose, with fond caress,
Stooped to touch a truant tress,
From her fillet struggling free,
Scorning its captivity.

IN AN OLD GARDEN.

There a bed of rue was set
With an edge of mignonette,
And the spicy bergamot
Meshed the frail forget-me-not.
Honeysuckles, hollyhocks,
Bachelor's-buttons, four-o'clocks,
Marigolds and blue-eyed-grass
Curtsied when the maid did pass.
Now the braggart weeds have spread
Through the paths she loved to tread,
And the creeping moss has grown
O'er yon shattered dial-stone.
Still beside the ruined walks
Some old flowers, on sturdy stalks,
Dream of her whose happy eyes
Roam the fields of Paradise.

SONNETS.

SONNETS.

A SEA GRAVE.

YEA, rock him gently in thine arms, O deep!
    No nobler heart was ever hushed to rest
Upon the chill, soft pillow of thy breast —
No truer eyes didst thou e'er kiss to sleep.
While o'er his couch the wrathful billows leap,
    And mighty winds roar from the darkened west,
Still may his head on thy cool weeds be pressed,
Far down where thou dost endless silence keep.
Oh, when, slow moving through thy spaces dim,
    Some scaly monster seeks its coral cave,
And pausing o'er the sleeper, stares with grim
    Dull eyes a moment downward through the wave,
Then let thy pale green shadows curtain him,
    And swaying sea-flowers hide his lonely grave.

VANISHED.

IT was but yesterday I saw his sheep,
    The while he led them up the height to feed,
And heard him merrily pipe upon his reed,
And mock the echoes from yon rocky steep;
'Twas yesterday I found him fast asleep,
    His flock forgot and wantoning in the mead,
    His pipe flung lightly by with idle heed,
And shadows lying round him, cool and deep.
But though I seek I shall not find him more,
    In dewy valley or on grassy height;
I listen for his piping — it is o'er,
    From out mine ears gone is the music quite;
There on the hill the sheep feed as before,
    But Pan, alas, has vanished from my sight!

SYRINX.

LEAVE me to wither here by this dark pool,
    Where the winds sigh and the shuddering reeds
  And slimy things creep through the water-weeds,
And snakes glide out from coverts dim and cool.
Leave me, O Pan; thou hast been made the fool
    Of thy hot love; go where thy white flock feeds,
  And pipe thy ditties in the dewy meads,
And watch the silly sheep that own thy rule.
Get hence; I am become a loveless thing;
    No charms of mine shall ever tempt thee more;
No more in valleys green and echoing
  Shalt thou surprise and fright me, as of yore;
Go, clash thy hoofs, and make the woodlands ring,
  But let me wither here on this dark shore.

CLEOPATRA TO ANTONY.

GO from me now ; I will no longer feel
    Your burning kisses on my fevered lips ;
You shall not hold one moment ev'n the tips
Of my shut fingers, though you cry and kneel.
My face aches, and my tired senses reel ;
    Through all my veins a drowsy poison slips
    My sight grows dim with gradual eclipse,
For slumber on mine eyes has set his seal.
Get hence ; I will no more to-night ; the bars
    Of love are placed against you now : go while
I hate you not, my Roman ; the sick stars
    Wax faint and pallid in the dawn's red smile.
Look ! I am quenched in sleep, as nenuphars
    Are quenched in the broad bosom of the Nile.

ROMEO TO JULIET.

LOVE, touch my mouth with kisses as with fire;
    Lean hard against my breast, that I may feel
From thy warm heart its influence subtly steal
Through all my veins; with overmuch desire
My spirit fainteth, and my lips suspire
    Swiftly with heavy breathings; round me reel
    The shadows of the dark, and downward whee
The dim, far stars from heaven; draw me nigher
Unto thy bosom, love, for all my sense
    Of earth and time fleets from me . . . Dayward
        flows
The stream of night, and into yon immense
    Blue void the slow moon fails; hold me more close,
Lest from thine arms my spirit hasten hence,
    Going that viewless way no mortal knows.

RIZPAH.

BLOWN through the gusty spaces of the night,
   The pale clouds fleet like ghosts along the sky ;
A fitful wind goes moaning feebly by,
And the faint moon, poised o'er the craggy height,
Dies in its own uncertain, misty light.
   Within the hills the water-springs are dry ;
   The herbs are withered ; and the sand-wastes lie
Dim, wide, and lonely to the weary sight.
Behold ! her awful vigil she will keep
   Through the wan night as through the burning day ;
Though all the world should sleep she will not sleep,
   But watch, wild-eyed and fierce, to scare away,
As round and round, with hoarse, low cries they creep,
   From her dead sons the hungry beasts of prey.

HAGAR.

WIDE wastes of sand beneath a burning sky;
   Far hills that shimmer in the breathless air;
  And clumps of stunted shrubs that, here and there,
With pale and parchèd leafage, vex the eye.
Her bread is spent, her water-skin is dry;
   The child's faint sobbings pierce her with despair;
   Her face is hid, her fallen head is bare;
"Now, O my God," she crieth, "let me die."
Hark! from the midmost heavens a deep sound:
   "What aileth thee? Rise, Hagar, fear thee not,
For God hath heard the child's voice from the ground,
   And he will succor thee in thy sore lot."
Then she arose, and took the lad, and found
   A crystal fountain in that desert spot.

SUNDERED.

I SHALL not touch her face, her hands again;
    I shall not mingle her warm breath with mine;
    I shall not drink again the nectared wine
Of her swift kisses, for dear Love is slain.
Yea, Love lies cold and dead; but pallid Pain,
    Upon whose haggard cheeks the salt tears shine,
    Hath set upon our brows her blood-red sign
Of hopeless anguish, like the mark of Cain.
Upon us Time hath wrought his change, for lo!
    Not now we meet and pass, as heretofore,
Each knowing that which none save us could know —
    How full of love our hearts were to the core;
But now across life's wide waste fields we go
    Our separate ways, to meet again no more.

CROESUS.

B.C. 546.

"O SOLON! Solon! wist ye of this hour,
    When midst the splendors that thine eyes did see,
    Undazzled by my gilded vanity,
Thou yet didst say how fleet is human power?
Lo! from this funeral pyre each flashing tower,
    Each sapphire dome, each gate of ivory,
    Makes all my court a hateful thing to me,
While here in death's grim shadow now I cower."

So Crœsus cried when fiery death was nigh,
    Remembering Solon's words of long ago;
Then the great Persian king, who paused hard by,
    Heared the sore wailing of his fallen foe,
And said: "Unbind him thence, he shall not die;
    Behold, one day I too shall be brought low!"

A CITY CRY.

HERE hoarsely moan the floods of human woe,
    And evermore, along the busy streets,
The iron hoof of traffic loudly beats,
And lean-faced avarice shuffles to and fro;
Here grudgingly the feet of mercy go
    Where gaunt and grimy squalor sits and eats
    Her bitter bread, and here, through foul retreats,
Death's noisome currents darkly ebb and flow.
O God, of those sweet airs which blow between
    The emerald hills, let me e'er breathe; keep me,
Far from the roaring city, in thy green
    And quiet solitudes, where I may see
The birds, the flowers, the grass, and sweetly lean
    My heart upon the peace and love of Thee.

THE PROPHET'S END.

BETTER to hide the weary face awhile ;
    Better to let them have it as they will ;
They would but mock thee, scourge thee, harry still
Thy tired soul ; go, cease thee from thy toil.
Flee from these dim vain ways where millions moil,
    And wrangle for a bauble ; let them fill
    Each other's restless lives with strenuous ill —
Thou shalt be free at last from strife and guile.
Go to thy mother, child, and take thy sleep ;
    Go, lay thee, silent, in her cool wide arms ;
Secure from troublous time, in her large keep
    Thou shalt lie peaceful 'mid the world's alarms ;
Go, get thee to thy mother-earth, and creep
    Into her bosom, where no evil harms.

THE TRAVELER.

WHEN in the dark we slowly drift away
    O'er unknown seas, and busy thoughts at last
  Are quieted, and all the cares are past
That, bandit-like, infest the realms of day —
To what pale country does the spirit stray?
  Within what wan-lit land, what region vast,
  Does this strange traveler journey far and fast,
Till in the east the day breaks, cold and gray?
Ah, tell me, when we slumber, whither goes,
  And whence at waking comes, the silent guest,
Whose face no man hath seen, whom no man knows —
  The dim familiar of each human breast?
Behold, at length, when day indeed shall close,
  Will this uneasy traveler, too, have rest?

THE ANGEL OF NIGHT.

WITH dusky pinions spread, from out the land
    Of twilight glides the angel of the night,
And earthward softly plumes her silent flight,
While gathering darkness from her wings is fanned
Across the cloud-world, musically and bland.
    Around her flow her garments, sprent with stars,
    As far away, toward the sunset bars,
She takes her noiseless flight, and from her hand
Scatters the balm of sleep on all below.
    From off her wings she winnows silver dew
On slumbering flowers, whose aromas go
    Far in Æolian wanderings, breaking through
Melodious silence in faint ebb and flow,
    Till fair Aurora peeps from eastern blue.

EDMUND SPENSER.

HOW have the years flown since that golden day
    When, where the Mulla rolls her dimpling flood,
Thou heardst the birds sing in the Irish wood,
And Raleigh with thee on the upland lay!
Again through gloomy forests old and gray,
    O'er many a waste and trackless solitude,
    Whithersoe'er thy Muse's knightly mood
May lead us in thy tale, we seem to stray.
O master, it was not on oaten reeds
    Thou madest music for the world's delight,
        Nor yet on Pan's shrill pipe didst thou e'er flute;
To sing of courtly grace and lordly deeds,
    Of lovely Una and the Redcross Knight,
        Behold! thou hadst Apollo's silver lute.

ADAM.

THE chaste young world gleamed round him; Paradise
　　All freshly radiant from the hand of God —
　　Its dewy ways by human feet untrod —
Revealed its virgin beauties to his eyes.
Above him soared the wondrous turquoise skies;
　　Beneath his feet rare flowers gemmed the sod;
　　And in the east he saw the morning, shod
With golden fire, behind the palms arise.

Not yet the tempter, with his honeyed wiles,
　　Had entered earth to vex the peace thereof,
But spicy airs roved through the vine-wreathed aisles,
　　And in the laurel cooed the turtle dove;
Still, cold and vain were Eden's balmiest smiles
　　To lonely Adam — lacking woman's love.

www.ingramcontent.com/pod-product-compliance
Lightning Source LLC
Chambersburg PA
CBHW020150170426
43199CB00010B/973